---- FOR A V

WITH AL

AUG

JOAN.

xxxx

Scarborough

in old picture postcards

by
Alan Pickup

European Library – Zaltbommel/Netherlands

Third edition: 1989

GB ISBN 90 288 2291 7 / CIP

© 1983 European Library – Zaltbommel/Netherlands

INTRODUCTION

The development of Scarborough reflects the changes which every other decade of holiday makers seem to demand, or at least those whose business it is to attract visitors, think they demand.

Originally the Old Town, which lay within the Bar, contained the old coaching inns such as the Bell on Bland's Cliff, the London, the George, and New Inn in Newborough and the Talbot and Blacksmith's Arms in Queen Street. It is hard to imagine Falsgrave as a village separated from the town by fields.

The Spa with its magical spring waters, which were considered a cure for almost any medical condition that the hypocondriacs considered they suffered from, was the great attraction. After the disasterous fire of 1876, the Spa was rebuilt and reopened in 1880 to cater for the requirements of the Victorian holiday makers by providing facilities for music, dancing, eating and walking.

With the arrival of the railway to Scarborough in 1845, this made the town much more accessible to the business folk from the West Riding and even further afield. Whereas the old coaches could bring less than a score of visitors at a time, the railway could transport them in vast numbers and far more quickly too. The next thirty years or so saw the boom in hotel building to cater for these new visitors, starting with the Crown in 1844. Others soon followed such as the Victoria, the Prince of Wales, the Alexandria, all named after Royalty, the Cambridge, the Grand in 1867 and the Pavilion in 1870. Now little more than one hundred years later, the Pavilion, the Balmoral and the Cambridge are only memories. There can be few folk who believe that the glass and concrete shop and office developments, which have replaced them, have in any way improved the architectural environment of the town. The trend today as far as holiday makers are concerned is for holiday flatlets, caravanning, self catering holidays and day trips.

Entertainment for the masses came with the underground aquarium in 1877 and although it later changed its name to The Peoples Palace and finally Gala Land, it provided a wealth of undercover entertainment by way of slide shows, penny slot machines and wax works which certainly provided shelter for visitors in times of wet weather all under one roof. The annual week's excursion to Scarborough became a reality for many more working class folk with the advent of paid holidays, however much it meant scimping and saving during the rest of the year.

In the period upto First World War open air entertainment was provided by way of Catlins Pierrots, band concerts and later the Fol de Rols at the Floral Hall.

The period between the wars saw the development era of the cinema with the Futurist, the Aberdeen, the Capital and finally the Odeon in 1938. Today, the town only has one regular cinema, but this is hardly surprising when most of the larger hotels can boast that every room has its own T.V. set, so that the guests do not have to set foot outside for their evening's entertainment.

It is perhaps hard to appreciate, seventy years on, the impact that the First World War made on the town. In the Second World War many of our larger cities and especially our industrial centres suffered from The Blitz.

However when the German navy sailed up the East Coast in 1914 and proceeded to shell the town, this was the first time for over one hundred years that anything like this had happened in this country. Not only had the town sent its fathers and sons to fight for their country, but in this instance the war had actually come to them. After shelling Scarborough on that November morning, the German ships continued sailing north and inflicted similar damage on Whitby and Hartlepools. The bombardment left nineteen dead and a further eighty wounded and property, including hotels, boarding houses, churches, chapels, schools and business premises, suffered extensive damage. King George V sent a message of sympathy to the town and the Mayor, Mr. C.C. Graham, suitably responded. No wonder the residents set about the task of raising funds, setting themselves a target of £185,000 for The Feed the Guns Campaign.

It was during the 1860's that Scarborough saw a great Church and chapel building extension programme. Today many of these buildings either do not exist at all or are no longer used for worship. Although the Primitive Methodist Chapel facade remains in St. John's Road, it is no longer a church and the same is true of the two Methodist churches on Seamer Road, which also served the Falsgrave communities. One is now a Jehovahs Witness Hall whilst the other is a judo club. The former red brick Anglican All Saints Church on Falsgrave has disappeared whilst the old Aberdeen Walk Methodist Church has been replaced by a super market now closed and the former Bar Congregational Church has been superseded by another modern shopping complex. These changes indicate both a movement of people out of the town centre and also a change in their Sunday habits too.

With the arrival of the age when almost every family has a motor car, it was inevitable that there should have been a decline in public transport facilities. The railway link north to Whitby went with the last passenger train in March 1965. The route westward to Pickering closed even earlier in June 1950 and there is constant talk of the line to Hull being under threat of closure.

The picture postcard collector is making a valuable contribution towards preserving the pictorial history of the town for the benefit of future generations.

About the Author

Mr. Alan Pickup has an extensive collection of old postcards and reproduction prints extending to over 6,000 items covering the towns and villages from Helmsley through to Scarborough with particular emphasis on Pickering, where he lives.

Acknowledgement

Almost all these cards have been obtained from, or made available to me by The Stamp Shop (stamps, postcards, coins, medals), 34, St. Nicholas Cliff, Scarborough, who do stock an extensive range of topographical cards of all parts of the country. Without their valued co-operation this book would not have been possible.

The Grand Roller Skating Rink, Scarborough.

1. The Grand Roller skating rink about 1909. The indoor roller skating rink was in Vernon Road and it was obviously a very popular sport at this period. Someone from Scarborough opened a similar rink in Pickering at the same time.

2. North Marine Road. Thomas E. Dent apart from being a grocer was also a wine and spirit merchant. The newsagents next door are advertising The Gazette, The Yorkshire Post, The Mirror and The Telegraph. They also operated a circulating library as did many newsagents in the days before there were public libraries.

Interior of Scarborough Station.

Scott Series. No 725

3. The interior of Scarborough station with its bookstall, Ladies rooms and the gas
lighting. The sad message on the reverse reads: 'The platform where I last saw my dear
mother, seeing me off to Doncaster 1906.'

NORTH BAY FROM CASTLE. SCARBOROUGH.

4. This view from the castle shows the North Pier before it was wrecked on 8th January 1905 and also the Warwick Revolving Tower, which went up in 1898 and was demolished in 1907 as it was considered unsightly. It boasted wonderful sea views from one hundred and fifty-five feet up.

5. Church Stairs Street in the Old Town leading up to St. Mary's Church, which can be seen in the background. The ladies are standing at the doors of their cottage, wearing the traditional long white aprons of the period. Leading off Church Stairs Street on the right is St. Mary's Place.

6. The new Salt Water Swimming Baths in 1906 complete with cafe at the corner of Blands Cliff and The Foreshore where Corrigan's Amusements are today. The baths were open daily, but on a Sunday only from 6 a.m. to 12 noon and admission was 6d. The Pictorial Photo Publishing Co were making a special offer: 'Your photos beautifully finished 12 for 1/- while you wait.'

7. This shows work in progress on the construction of the North Marine Drive. Although the work commenced in 1896, it was not finally completed until 1908 due in the main to problems created by gales and rough seas, which made progress very hazardous.

PRINCESS PATRICIA

OPENING MARINE DRIVE SCARBOROUGH

8. Scarborough's two and a half mile seafront road was finally completed with the opening of the Marine Drive by Princess Patricia, seen arriving from her carriage in this picture. Work had first begun on the Marine Drive in 1896, but the work was not completed until 1908. A picture is in existance showing them lowering the final block into position.

9. The Spa after it was rebuilt in 1880 after a disasterous fire in 1876. It was designed by
Thomas Verity. At one time the Spa complex was privately owned, but the Town Council
took over in 1957. The building on the horizon at the right is The Crown Hotel.

10. Work underway widening the Valley Bridge to its present width. The task took three years to complete and the new bridge was officially opened in 1928. Until 1919 the old bridge had been a toll bridge.

11. The procession which was held to mark the opening of the New Valley Bridge, which was opened on July 26th, 1928 by Mrs. Wilfred Ashley. The bridge consists of four spans one hundred and fifty feet each and provided a roadway forty feet wide with two footpaths of over twelve feet each and the approximate cost of the widening was £158,000 and the work took three years to complete. In the background is the now demolished Cambridge Hotel.

THE NEW VALLEY BRIDGE, SCARBOROUGH.
Opened by Mrs. WILFRID ASHLEY, July 26th, 1928.

12. This shows the damage to the Spa caused by a storm on March 12th, 1906. Here workmen can be seen inspecting the damage. Some idea of the force of the storm can be gained from the huge size of the stone blocks involved.

13. The Victoria Fruit Market. Both the barrow and the flat cart belonged to E. Lazonby & Co, Potato Merchants. It was very common to display merchandise outside on the pavement at this period. Hanging up are rabbits although one would have associated these with a butcher's business. Next door Webster's the Chemists proudly proclaimed 'Prescriptions accurately dispensed'.

14. The Mayor's car with his chauffer proudly standing by in his uniform. One would assume that he would not have to be in too much of a hurry getting to functions in this vehicle. It is interesting to know that the number plate AJ1 remains the number plate of the Chief Constable of North Yorkshire!

15. Will Catlin rebuilt Catlins Arcadia as an open air Pierrot theatre in 1909. It had originally been opened in 1903 as Kiralfy's Arcadia, which was a fun palace. In 1911 he replaced the Sheffield Arms, which can be seen on the extreme right with The Arcadian Restaurant.

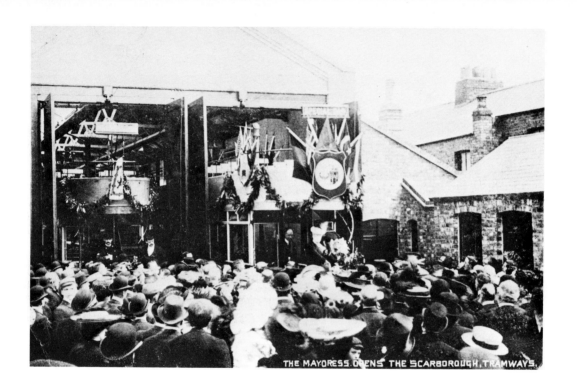

THE MAYORESS OPENS THE SCARBOROUGH TRAMWAYS.

16. For a period of twenty-seven years, until 1931, trams were to play an important part in the life of both residents and visitors alike as few folk possessed transport of their own, unless it was a push bike, at this time. This shows the official opening of the Tramway Depot by The Mayoress in 1904.

17. All Saints Church on Falsgrave in 1908, covered with what looks like virinia creeper. This Church has been pulled down and a housing complex occupies the site now. Next door in this picture is a shoe shop and the young sapling trees have wooden structures round them to protect them from damage by horses.

18. This Westborough Street scene of about 1907 shows the entrance to The Londesborough Theatre and the production seems to be called 'Quality Street'. Next to this is Bentley's Fancy Good's Shop, a hairdressers and then a sweet shop. On the extreme right is the Industrial Home for Blind Women. On the other side of the theatre is Sinfield's Tobacconists. Horse-drawn vehicles out number cars by seven to two.

PEASHOLME LAKE, SCARBOROUGH.

Fenton's Series

19. Peasholm Park was opened in 1912 on what had previously been Tucker's Field and in 1924 Peaseholm Glen was added. This picture shows the island in the middle of Peaseholm Lake, but without any trees on it and the entire site seems very bare and open compared with today. Oliver's Mount in the distance is without its War Memorial.

20. A naval procession coming down Vernon Road sometime after 1904. The flat cart going up Vernon Road belongs to J. Slater, Nurseryman. The tram is bound for Scalby Road and crowds are lining the Grand Hotel Square to watch the parade.

21. Looking along St. Nicholas Street about 1910 with Boots Chemists dominating the corner and further along Marshall & Snelgroves premises. Far more shops had sun blinds to protect their goods from fading by the sun than is the case today. This card was produced by Boots Cash Chemists.

PROCLAMATION OF KING GEORGE V AT SCARBORO' MAY 10ᵀᴴ 19

THE MAYOR AND CORPORATION BEFORE THE CEREMON

22. The official civic party led by the Mayor and accompanied by the Town Clerk resplendent in his wig marching in the Town Hall Gardens on St. Nicholas Street to read the formal Proclamation of the accession of King George V to the throne on May 10th, 1910. This event was repeated up and down the country.

23. The Rose and Crown Hotel is still in existance today, but it seems extremely doubtful if they will still be supplying Bass's Ales at 2/3d per dozen or Guinness's Stout at only 2/- a dozen and Old Port from 3/- to 5/- per bottle!

24. The unveiling of the Queen Victoria Memorial Statue in the Town Hall Gardens by Her Royal Highness Princess Henry of Battenberg (Princess Beatrice) on July 28th, 1903.

25. The Grand Hotel which was built in 1867 and at that time was described as 'the largest and most handsome in Europe'. It replaced various lodging houses which previously occupied this site. The hotel is now part of the Butlin empire. Just off the picture to the left is The Stamp Shop, which has supplied most of the postcards for this book.

26. The Fish Market in 1906 with the carts waiting to be loaded. The Lord Nelson Hotel, which is still there today, is taking delivery of crates of beer by horse and cart. The building on the left of the Foreshore, with the small balcony, belongs to the Amateur Rowing Club.

27. The Aquarium and Peoples Palace in 1907. The complex was originally built in late 1870's, then it became Gala Land and then, a hundred years later, it became an underground car park. The hotel looking over this amusement centre is the Esplanade Boarding Establishment.

28. Hopper and Mason's shop in Westborough specially decorated to mark the visit of Princess Beatrice to Scarborough in July 1903 to unveil the statue to Queen Victoria in the Town Hall gardens. Today this site is occupied by Boots Chemists.

29. The Old Ship Inn in Falsgrave in 1906. The pub is still there today, but it is called just The Ship Inn. It is a lady driving the pony and cart and the young tree has wooden fencing around it to protect it from damage by horses. The lady is Ada Horsney and the cart was known as 'the Seamer Express'.

30. These horses and carts are taken down by the Pier with St. Mary's Church in the background. On the pier are stacked lots of barrels. As Scarborough had several breweries at this time, all producing their own ale, it is possible that this is what these contain.

31. Tonk's shop in Westborough decorated with garlands and bunting in 1910 to mark the Coronation of George V. Since they closed and the premises have been bought by Littlewood's, they have remained empty and waiting for re-development.

SCARBOROUGH'S MUNICIPAL SCHOOLS.

32. Scarborough's Municipal Schools. This most imposing building was later to become the Scarborough Boys High School and then when it moved to new premises, Theatre in the Round took over. They certainly don't build schools like this anymore. This card is certainly pre-1918. One of the drawbacks of having a school on a hill side was that there were no playing fields adjacent. The High School playing fields were at the top of Oliver's Mount. I recall travelling from Pickering by train and then having to walk from the station to Oliver's Mount taking it in turns to carry the cricket bag. No wonder we were worn out before a ball was bowled.

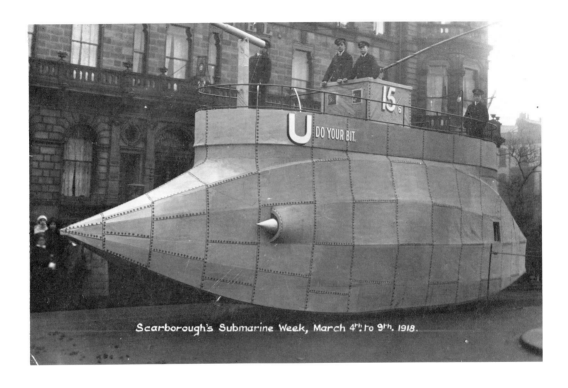

Scarborough's Submarine Week, March 4th to 9th 1918.

33. This model with the inscription 'U do your bit' was to mark Scarborough's Submarine Week March 4th to 9th in 1918. This is taken in front of the former Pavilion Hotel. A similar card exists with a model taken in the same position with the words 'Feed the Guns Remember Scarborough'. This latter campaign was from November 11th to 16th, 1918. The reverse of this submarine card had a printed verse entitled All aboard for the submarine urging folk to give generously for the War Effort and was produced on behalf of the National War Bond Campaign.

34. The old Lighthouse which was so badly damaged by the German bombardment of 1914 that it required pulling down and rebuilding when the war was over. Sidney Smith of Pickering apparently also produced a series of cards covering the properties damaged in the bombardment, but so far only a single card No. 6, Damage to New Co operative stores, has been traced.

35. On December 16th, 1914 the German Navy shelled the town killing nineteen residents and wounding a further eighty. A whole series of cards was produced covering all the properties damaged. This one is of 79, Commercial Street. It was estimated that as many as five hundred shells were fired.

SCARBOROUGH. IN THE VALLEY.

PUBLISHED &
SOLD AT ROWNTREES CAFE, SCARBOROUGH.

36. This card was one of a series produced for advertisement purposes by Rowntrees Cafe, each had a printed message on the back. This one reads: 'Right in the centre of the town is the Valley Park with its ornamental lake on which ducks, geese and swans reside. We like to sit here and then go for afternoon tea to Rowntrees Cafe.'

SCARBOROUGH — SCALBY MILLS.

37. The Scalby Mills Hotel as it was in 1904 in a beautiful tranquil setting long before any commercial development took place. This card was chosen for printing as a private Xmas card on the reverse from Mr. & Mrs. J.W. Sutton of Raincliffe View, Lyell Street and posted on December 24th, so that it would be delivered Xmas morning.

38. Queen's Parade just after the turn of the century in the era of the cab and the pony and trap, when for either a lady or a gentleman to be out without something on their head was considered to be indecently dressed!

IN RAMSDALE VALLEY, SCARBOROUGH.

39. This is the scene in 1906 looking down the Ramsdale Valley with an open topped tram negotiating the corner. It must have been quite a pull up here as it is quite steep. It was across the Ramsdale Valley that Sir Joseph Paxton's Westbourne development commenced in 1862.

North Bay, Scarborough

40. This scene, taken at the North Bay, is before January 1905 as the North Pier can be seen. The Royal Albert Drive was opened in 1890 by the Duke of Clarence. This shows a close up of the bathing huts, which were a traditional feature of the British seaside scene of this period. There is also what looks like a barrel organ.

The Pierrots, South Sands.   Scarborough.

41. This shows the crowded beach in front of the Spa watching a performance of The Pierrots, but there is not a naked body in sight. It is before 1907 as the Warwick Revolving Tower can be seen on the horizon. Note the bathing huts actually in the sea.

Scarborough-Mere & Olivers' Mount

42. This shows the Mere and in the background Oliver's Mount at about the turn of the century in a completely rural setting without any housing in sight, the only building being the wooden boat house and without the War Memorial dominating the horizon.

43. The War Memorial taken in the early 1920's. Errected to commemorate those who had given their lives in the First World War and which today still dominates Oliver's Mount. This vantage point gives wonderful views over the whole town.

The Municipal Buildings, Scarborough

44. Many people probably imagine that the red brick Town Hall building in St. Nicholas Street is a relatively modern building. They will be surprised to see it in this Edwardian setting with a horse and carriage; with the coachman complete in top hat; driving passed. It is worth noting the total absence of public seats on the pavement at this time.

SCARBOROUGH, ENTRANCE TO SPA.

45. This shows the entrance to the Cliff Bridge which leads to the Spa in about 1909. In about 1826 the Cliff Bridge Company leased the Spa from the Corporation and erected the iron bridge. When this bridge was a toll bridge in private ownership, stories are told of them taking pennies by the barrow load to the bank daily!

46. West Square with the station clock tower on the right and the demolished Pavilion Hotel just peeping out beside Matson's Boarding House. This building has been demolished, but the other properties remain. The grassed area with the rockery in the centre now contains a lily pond.

47. The Scotch fisher girls seen at Scarborough in 1907. Scottish fishing boats continued to make an annual call at Scarborough for about a further sixty years as they followed the seasonal movement of herring shoals down the north east coast.

Scotch Fisher Girls at Scarborough.

CHAS. GADDY'S COACH THE "VIVID"
(Awarded First Prize for the Smartest Turnout in the District 1907, 1908, and 1909.)
LEAVES THE GRAND HOTEL SQUARE DAILY FOR THE PRINCIPAL DRIVES AT 10-30 A.M AND 2-30 P.M
Seats may be booked at Messrs. Ruddock Bros., Wine and Spirit Merchants, Grand Hotel Square.
ADDRESS : ALBEMARLE MEWS, SCARBOROUGH.

48. Charles Gaddy's Coach 'The Vivid'. This was awarded the first prize for the smartest turn out in the district in 1907, 1908 and 1909. The coach left the Grand Hotel Square daily at 10.30 a.m. and 2.30 p.m. for tours. Seats could be booked in advance at Messrs. Ruddock Bros Wine & Spirit Merchants in Grand Hotel Square.

49. The Royal Northern Sea Bathing Infirmary as it was then called. Today it is still serving the sick as St. Thomas convalescent Hospital. It has wonderful sea views, but with all the continual traffic and the amusement arcades around it, patients must find it rather noisy.

WESTBOROUGH, SCARBOROUGH

50. Looking up Westborough pre-1914 with the Bar Church on the right. There are still more horses and carts and traps than cars in sight! The trams continued to run until 1931 and here one can see the tram lines from Aberdeen Walk going down Vernon Road. After the era of the trams some of the poles which had carried the cables were converted to take street lights. This tram carries an advert for The Londesborough Theatre, which became a cinema in 1914 and was demolished in 1959.

Scarborough.
Clarence Gardens. Bandstand.

51. The cliffs below The Queen's Parade were converted in the period pre-1890 into the Clarence Gardens and band concerts were held in the band stand. This picture, dated about 1900, shows four young gentlemen out for a stroll, two of them with walking sticks. It must have been extremely hot as numerous ladies have parasols up to shade them from the sun.

SCARBOROUGH - BLENHEIM TERRACE.

52. Blenheim Terrace in 1905 thronged with Edwardian holiday makers, all dressed out in their finery. The fronts of these properties were gardens at this time, but now many of them have been concreted over to make hard standing for visitors cars.

53. This is Church Stairs Street showing the old cottages, which stood in this part of the old town until they were demolished about 1930 with St. Mary's Parish Church behind.

CASTLE HILL, FROM HARBOUR, SCARBOROUGH.

54. This view of the Castle Hill from the Harbour was taken in 1909 and shows the entrance to the Marine Drive long before Corrigan's Fun Fair appeared on the scene.

55. King Richard III's House where he is reputed to
have lived in 1484. The house was built about 1350
and was restored in 1914 and is now a museum containing interesting old curios, furniture and bygonnes
situated on the Foreshore.

56. The Old Bar, which was demolished in December 1890. The Old Bar public house became The Huntsman when it became a Tetley House. The shops next to it were demolished to gain entry to North Street. It was from this old bar that the Congregational Church on the corner of Westborough and Aberdeen Walk took its name. Following the demolition of the bar, the Bull Hotel was rebuilt in 1891 and later became the Balmoral Hotel.

ST MARYS CHURCH & CASTLE
SCARBOROUGH.

57. St. Mary's Parish Church with the castle in the background, taken in 1905. In the church yard is Ann Bronte's grave. She died in 1849 in the cottages which stood on the site of the present Grand Hotel, which was opened in 1867.

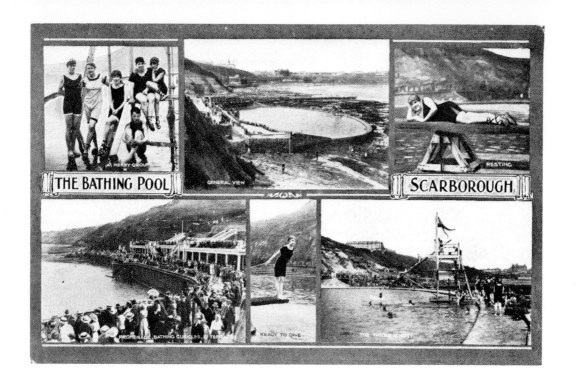

THE BATHING POOL

A MERRY GROUP

GENERAL VIEW

SCARBOROUGH

RESTING

PROMENADE, BATHING CUBICLES, & TERRACE

READY TO DIVE

THE WATER SHOOT

58. These shots of the open air bathing pool beyond the Spa at the South Bay are of the 1920 period. This was the only bathing pool until the North Bay Pool was opened in 1938. The long one piece costumes these young ladies are wearing are in marked contrast to the bikinis of today. The South bathing pool was opened in 1914, but was only for the hardy as it was unheated.

SCARBOROUGH, SPA TERRACE

59. This view of the Spa and the terraced gardens, showing ladies and their escourts sampling the sea air, reminds us of the genteel age of the Edwardians. This scene is pre-1906.

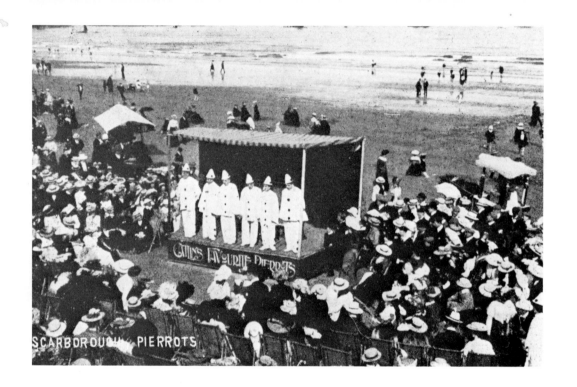

60. Here Catlin's Pierrots are giving an open air performance on the South Foreshore beach. Kiralfy's Arcadia was a fun palace, which opened in 1903 at the foot of Blands Cliff and then Will Catlin rebuilt it as an open air pierrot theatre in 1909. Today the Futurist Theatre occupies the site.

61. The Royal procession containing the Duke and Duchess of Connaught proceeds up Westborough following the official opening of the Marine Drive in 1908. The buildings in the background are the present Co op and the Electricity Board showrooms.

THE SCARBOROUGH PAGEANT. 1912. EPISODE 9.

62. 1912 was the year for historic pageants and naturally the castle grounds was the obvious choice of venue. In 1910 Pickering put on a similar event in its castle grounds. This card is one of a whole series covering the various scenes and the castle makes an impressive back cloth.

Scarborough, Westborough, 1891

28817

63. Looking down Westborough in 1891 from the corner of Aberdeen Walk. On the left is the Bar Congregational Church, which was demolished to make way for the modern shopping block. On the right is The Railway Hotel, which seems a long way from the railway station, and opposite is Graham's Adelphi Commercial Hotel.

64. A thriving Westborough with boarding houses above the shops. This open topped tram must have been one of the earliest as they made their first appearance in 1904 and this card was postmarked 1905.

65. Quay Street in what was originally the heart of the old town as it was in 1908. Centuries before, as its name implies, this street formed the boundary of the harbour. At one time the Town Hall stood on the site of the present Bethel Fisherman's Chapel.

SCARBOROUGH RAILWAY STATION.

66. The Railway station with its forecourt enclosed by iron railings with a pony and trap where the taxis stand today. Behind stands the imposing Pavilion Hotel, built in 1870 and which closed in 1971 to be demolished to make way for a glass and concrete office block.

67. This is the lifeboat 'Edward & Lucille' at the turn of the century, when it was stationed at the foot of St. Nicholas Cliff. The minaret behind is part of the Sea Water Baths, which were at the foot of Blands Cliff.

68. In the period upto 1910, the North Eastern Railway had a fleet of these chara bancs for carrying visitors on tours of the area. This one is seen setting off from the railway station for Forge Valley. Local photographers would take a picture as the passengers set off and have proof copies ready by the time the chara returned to obtain orders.

69. This card, showing freak waves pounding the Spa, seems an odd choice to send as a private greetings card for Xmas 1905, but it was the selection of Mrs. & Miss Webster of 62, Victoria Road. When the picture postcard was first legalised in 1894, the postage rate was ½d and it remained at this rate until June 1918.

70. The scene of the Great Fire of February 26th, 1915, which destroyed Boyes Remnant Warehouse in Market Street and also completely gutted Queen Street Methodist Chapel next door.

71. A special stage coach service called The Venture commenced between Scarborough & Harrogate on 2nd July 1900 and continued for some three years. The booking office was at The Grand Hotel. The single fare was 15/- and the coach left at 10.30 a.m., arriving at 6.30. It operated on alternative days of the week in each direction.

Burniston Baptist Picnic July 1 25   3850

72. This open coach is taking members of the then thriving Baptist Church at Burniston on their annual picnic outing on July 1st, 1925. There is also in existance an interior shot of the church decorated with Harvest produce in 1923. The church closed down a few years ago.

73. The North Pier was opened in July 1869. This shows the wreck of the pier after it had been destroyed by a storm on 7th January 1905. It was never rebuilt.

74. The old Valley Bridge, which was originally a toll bridge, and the buildings either side were the toll booths. The bus indicator reads 'Town & South Cliff, Holbeck Gardens, penny fares'. At this time the two buildings were kiosks, selling papers, postcards and sweets.

75. This reminds us of 'Those men in their magnificent flying machines'. This Daily Mail sponsored light aircraft is seen on the beach at Whitsuntide 1914 where it proved a great attraction. Those who flew these machines were either extremely brave souls or as some would say very foolhardy. In later years Sopwith Sea planes made their appearance in the bay.

76. The Ramshill Hotel, South Cliff in 1905 with three coaches and horses waiting for passengers with the coachmen dressed in black top hats. These coaches plied for hire in the same way that taxis do today. It must have been much more exciting, in fine weather at least, riding in style in one of these. The sender of this card had wanted to get a real photo card of the North Pier gale damage, but they had apparantly sold out a month later.